Science Safety Rules

by Kelli Hicks

Science Content Editor:
Kristi Lew

Educational Media

rourkeeducationalmedia.com

Science content editor: Kristi Lew

A former high school teacher with a background in biochemistry and more than 10 years of experience in cytogenetic laboratories, Kristi Lew specializes in taking complex scientific information and making it fun and interesting for scientists and non-scientists alike. She is the author of more than 20 science books for children and teachers.

www.rourkeeducationalmedia.com

Photo credits:
Cover © Michael J Thompson; Cover logo frog © Eric Pohl, test tube © Sergey Lazarev; Page 3 © Rob Marmion; Page 5 © Noam Armonn; Page 7 © StockLite; Page 9 © StockLite; Page 11 © Rob Marmion; Page 13 © Tomasz Trojanowski; Page 15 © Jeanne Hatch; Page 17 © andrzej80; Page 19 © mick20; Page 20 © Morgan Lane Photography; Page 22 © Jeanne Hatch, Piotr Marcinski, Rob Marmion; Page 23 © greenland, Michael Chamberlin, Morgan Lane Photography

Editor: Jeanne Sturm

Cover and page design by Nicola Stratford, bdpublishing.com

Library of Congress Cataloging-in-Publication Data

Hicks, Kelli L.
 Science safety rules / Kelli Hicks.
    p. cm. -- (My science library)
 Includes bibliographical references and index.
 ISBN 978-1-61741-730-6 (Hard cover) (alk. paper)
 ISBN 978-1-61741-932-4 (Soft cover)
 1. Science--Experiments--Safety measures--Juvenile literature. 2. Laboratories--Safety measures--Juvenile literature. I. Title.
 Q182.3.H53 2011
 502.8'9--dc22
                                    2011003763

Rourke Educational Media
Printed in the United States of America,
North Mankato, Minnesota

rourkeeducationalmedia.com

customerservice@rourkeeducationalmedia.com • PO Box 643328 Vero Beach, Florida 32964

Do you want to be
a **scientist**?

Scientists follow rules
to stay safe.

Rule #1

Listen and follow
the directions.

Rule #2

Wash your **hands** before you begin.

Rule #3

Wear **goggles** to cover your eyes.

Rule #4

Use your eyes and **ears**, but never taste or smell.

Rule #5

Treat all **animals** in the **lab** with care.

Rule #6

Always walk in the lab.

Rule #7

Clean up your area.

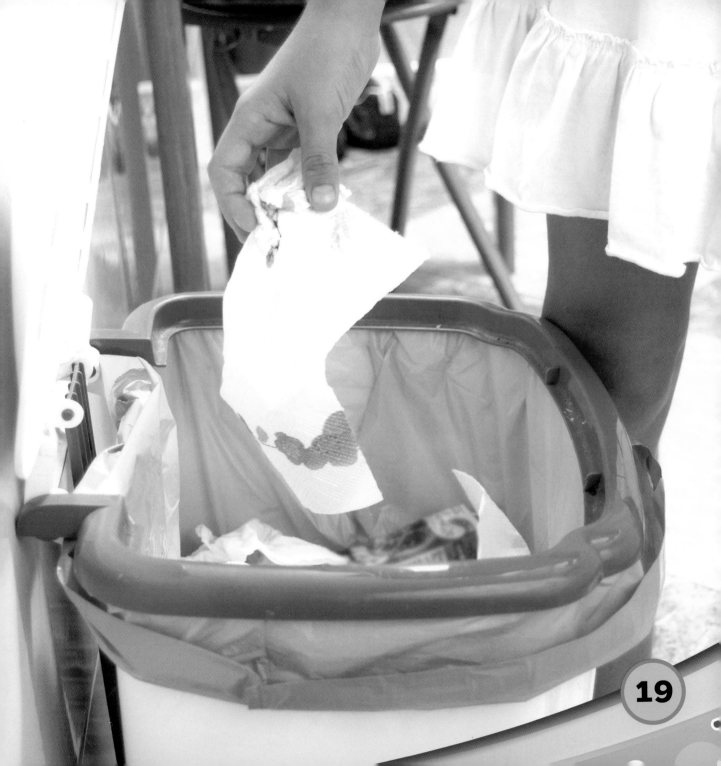

19

Follow the safety rules and you can be a scientist, too!

SHOW what you know

1. How do you show you care about an animal?

2. Why should you wear goggles?

3. What would happen if you ran in the science lab?

Picture Glossary

animals (AN-uh-muhlz):
Animals are any living creatures that breathe and move about.

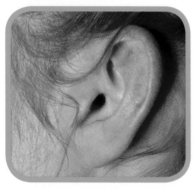

ears (IHRZ):
Ears are the parts of the body used to hear.

goggles (GOG-uhlz):
Goggles are special glasses that fit tightly around your eyes to protect them.

hands (HANDZ):
Hands are the body parts on the ends of your arms.

lab (LAB):
Short for laboratory, a lab is a room or building that has special equipment for science experiments.

scientist (SYE-uhn-tist):
A scientist is a person who does tests to learn about our world.

Index

Websites

www.sciencenewsforkids.org/pages/safetyzone.asp

www.sciencelabsafety.net

www.kids-science-experiments.com/lab-rules.html

About the Author

Kelli Hicks loves writing about sports, science, and the fun things her large family likes to do. She loves to learn about science and always tries to follow the rules to stay safe. She lives in Tampa with her husband, two children Mackenzie and Barrett, and their golden retriever Gingerbread.